STANDING
IN THE GAP

"I looked for a man who would build up the wall and stand before Me in the gap on behalf of the land."
EZEKIEL 22:30

ANDREW MURRAY

CHRISTIAN ART
PUBLISHERS

Published by Christian Art Publishers
PO Box 1599, Vereeniging, 1930, RSA

© 2008
First edition 2008

Cover designed by Christian Art Publishers

Cover Image © Sean Elliott, 2007
Used under license from Shutterstock.com.

Set in 11 on 14 pt New Century Schoolbook by
Christian Art Publishers

Printed in China

ISBN 978-1-77036-052-5

08 09 10 11 12 13 14 15 16 17 – 10 9 8 7 6 5 4 3 2 1

CONTENTS

INTRODUCTION

This little book has been prepared with the view of rousing Christians to some right sense of the solemn duty, the high privilege, and the wonderful power of intercession.

It seeks to point out what place intercession has in God's plan for the extension of His kingdom, and for the strengthening of the life of His children so that they may receive from Him the heavenly blessings He has to bestow and then go forth to impart them to the world around them.

The Dutch original has encouraged Christians to realize their high calling and has helped them to take their place among those who remember the Lord and who call upon Him day and night.

This translation is issued with the hope and prayer that it may be used by individuals as well as in Bible classes and prayer meetings to foster that spirit of devotion and prayer that is so essential to the Christian life.

ANDREW MURRAY

CHAPTER 1

Intercession

Pray for each other.

~ James 5:16 ~

What a mystery of glory there is in prayer! On the one hand we see God in His holiness, love, and power waiting and longing to bless man. On the other hand there is sinful man, a worm of the dust, bringing down from God by prayer the very life and love of heaven to dwell in his heart.

But the glory of intercession is so much greater – when a man is bold and asks from God what he desires for others. He seeks to bring to one soul, or maybe hundreds and thousands, the power of the eternal life with all its blessings.

Intercession! Surely this is the very holiest exercise of our boldness as God's children? It is the highest privilege and enjoyment connected to our communion with God. It is the power of being used by God as an instrument for His great work of making people His dwelling place and showing forth His glory.

Surely the church should count intercession as one of the chief means of grace? The church should seek, above everything else, to cultivate in God's children the power of an unceasing prayerfulness on behalf of the perishing world.

Believers who have to some extent been brought into the secret should know what strength there is in unity. And what assurance there is that God will avenge His people who cry to Him day and night.

It is only when Christians stop looking for help in external union and bind together as one to the throne of God through an unceasing devotion to Jesus Christ and an unceasing continuance in supplication for the power of God's Spirit, that the church will put on her beautiful garments and her strength, too, and overcome the world.

Our Gracious Father,

Hear our prayer and teach Your church, and each of us, what is the glory, what is the blessing, what is the all prevailing power of intercession.

We pray that You will give us the vision of what intercession means to You, so that we might carry out Your blessed purpose – what it means to ourselves as the exercise of our royal priesthood, and what it will mean to Your church, and to perishing men, in the bringing down of the Spirit in power – for Jesus' sake.

Amen.

Stand in the gap

The glory of intercession is when a person is bold and asks from God what he desires for others.

CHAPTER 2

Open Eyes

And Elisha prayed, "O LORD, open his eyes, that he may see."

Elisha said, "LORD, open the eyes of these men so they can see."

~ 2 Kings 6:17, 20 ~

How wonderfully the prayer of Elisha for his servant was answered! The young man saw the mountain full of chariots of fire and horsemen around Elisha. The heavenly host had been sent by God to protect His servant.

A second time Elisha prayed. The Syrian army had been struck by blindness and led into Samaria. There Elisha prayed for the opening of their eyes, and they discovered they were hopeless prisoners in the hand of the enemy.

Let us use these prayers in our own prayers. Firstly, to ask that our eyes may see the wonderful provision that God has made for His church in the outpouring of the Holy Spirit. All the powers of heaven are at our disposal.

How little the children of God live in the faith of that heavenly vision – the power of the Holy Spirit on them, with them, and in them, for their own spiritual lives and as their strength to joyfully witness for the Lord and His work!

But that second prayer is important too, that God may open the eyes of His children who do not yet see the power that the world and sin have upon them. They are unaware of the weakness that marks the church, which makes it helpless in winning souls for Christ and building up believers for a life of holiness and fruitfulness.

Let us pray that God may open all eyes to see what the great and fundamental need of the church is, so that the power of the Spirit may be known unceasingly in its divine ability and blessing.

Our Heavenly Father,

You who are so unspeakably willing to give us Your Holy Spirit in power, hear our humble prayer.

Open our eyes that we may realize fully the low estate of Your church and people, yet just as fully what treasures of grace and power You are willing to bestow in answer to the fervent prayer of a united church.

Amen.

Stand in the Gap

Pray for God to open your eyes
to see the power of the Holy Spirit
and the need of the church.

CHAPTER 3

Man's Place in God's Plan

The highest heavens belong to the LORD, but the earth He has given to man.

~ Psalm 115:16 ~

God created heaven as a dwelling place for Himself – perfect, glorious, and most holy. He gave the earth to man to live in – everything very good in the beginning, but it needed to be kept and cultivated. It was man's responsibility to continue and perfect the work God had done.

Think of the iron and the coal hidden away in the earth, of the steam hidden away in the water.

It was left to man to discover these things and to use them, like we see in the network of railways that span the world and the ships that cross the ocean.

God created everything to be used. He made the discovery and the use dependent on the wisdom and diligence of man. What the earth is today, with its cities and houses, with its cornfields and orchards, it owes to man. The work God had begun and prepared was to be carried out by man in fulfillment of God's purpose. And so nature teaches us the wonderful partnership to which God calls us for the carrying out of the work of creation to its destined end.

This law holds true in the kingdom of grace too. In this great redemption God has revealed the power of the heavenly life and the spiritual blessings of which heaven is full. But He has entrusted to His people the work of making these blessings known and making people partakers of them.

What diligence the children of this world show in seeking the treasures that God has hidden in the earth for their use! As children of God we should be equally faithful in seeking the treasures hidden in heaven, to bring them down in blessing on the world.

It is through the unceasing intercession of God's people that His kingdom will come, and His will be done on earth as in heaven (Matt. 6:10).

Ever Blessed Lord,

How wonderful is the place You have given man. Thank You for trusting us to continue the work You began.

We pray that You will open our hearts to the great thought that, through the preaching of the gospel, and the work of intercession, Your people are to work out Your purpose. Lord, open our eyes, for Jesus' sake.

Amen.

Stand in the gap

Pray that God's kingdom shall come,
that His will be done on earth.

CHAPTER 4

Intercession in the Plan of Redemption

O You who hear prayer, to You all men will come.

~ Psalm 65:2 ~

When God gave power to man, who was created in His own image, to govern the world under Him, it was His plan that Adam should do nothing except that which was with God and through God. God Himself would do all His work in the world through Adam. Adam was to be the owner, master, and ruler of the earth.

When sin entered the world, however, Adam's power proved to be a terrible reality. It was through him that the earth, and the whole race of man, was brought under the curse of sin.

When God made the plan of redemption, His object was to restore man to his former position. God chose His servants of old who, through the power of intercession, could ask for what they wanted and it would be given to them.

When Christ became man, it was so that, as man, both on earth and in heaven, He might intercede for mankind. Before He left the world, He imparted this right of intercession to His disciples, in the sevenfold promise of His farewell discourse (John 15-17), that whatever they asked for, He would do.

God's intense longing to bless is in some sense limited by His dependence on the intercession that rises from the earth. He seeks to rouse the spirit of intercession so that He can bestow His blessing on mankind.

God regards intercession as the highest expression of His people's readiness to receive and to yield themselves wholly to the working of His almighty power.

Christians need to recognize intercession as their true nobility and their only power with God — the right to claim and expect that God will hear their prayers. It is only as God's children begin to see what intercession means in regard to God's kingdom that they will realize how important their responsibility is.

As they understand what intercession means each individual believer will be led to see that God waits for him to take his part. Believers should feel that the highest, the most blessed, the mightiest of all human instrumentalities for the fulfillment of "on earth as it is in heaven" (Matt. 6:10), is the intercession that rises day and night.

Christian warriors are pleading with God for the power of heaven to be sent down into the hearts of people. May God burn this one thought into our hearts: Intercession in its omnipotent power is according to His will and is most effectual!

Father,

Thank You for the gift of intercession. Help us to rise up as warriors and pray day and night so that the fulfillment of the Word may come to pass, "on earth as it is in heaven."

Amen.

Stand in the gap

Intercession is your true nobility
and only power with God.

CHAPTER 5

God Seeks Intercessors

He saw that there was no man, and wondered that there was no intercessor.

~ Isaiah 59:16 KJV ~

From the start God had intercessors among His people, people to whose voice He listened and gave deliverance to. In Isaiah 59 we read of a time of trouble when God sought for an intercessor in vain. *And He wondered!* Think of what that means – that God was amazed that there was no-one who loved the people enough or who had sufficient faith in God's power to deliver, to intercede on their behalf.

If there had been an intercessor God would have given the people deliverance, but without an intercessor His judgments came down (see Isa. 64:7; Ezek. 22:30-31).

The intercessor holds such an important place in the kingdom of God! It's a matter of wonder that God should give people such power. Yet, there are so few who know what it is to take hold of His strength and pray down His blessing on the world.

Let us try to realize the position. When God had in His Son wrought out the new creation and Christ had taken His place on the throne, the work of the extension of His kingdom was given into the hands of men. He ever lives to pray.

Prayer is the highest exercise of Christ's royal prerogative as Priest-King upon the throne. All that Christ was to do in heaven was to be in fellowship with His people on earth.

In His divine condescension God has willed that the working of His Spirit shall follow the prayers of His people. He waits for their intercession, which shows the preparation of their hearts, to see to what extent they are ready to yield to His Spirit's control.

God rules the world and His church through the prayers of His people. That God made the extension of His kingdom largely dependent on the faithfulness of His people in prayer is an amazing mystery and yet an absolute certainty. God calls for intercessors: in His grace He has made His work dependent on them. He waits for them.

Our Father,

Open our eyes to see that You invite Your children to have a part in the extension of Your kingdom by their faithfulness in prayer and intercession.

Give us such an insight into the glory of this holy calling that we may yield ourselves to its blessed service with our whole hearts.

Amen.

Stand in the gap

God is waiting to hear your prayers.

CHAPTER 6

Christ as Intercessor

Therefore He is able to save completely those who come to God through Him, because He always lives to intercede for them.

~ Hebrews 7:25 ~

In Isaiah, when God wondered that there was no intercessor, these words followed, "therefore His arm brought salvation unto Him" (Isa. 59:16 KJV). "The Redeemer will come to Zion" (Isa. 59:20). God Himself would provide the true intercessor, in Christ His Son, of whom it had already been said, "He bore the sin of many, and made intercession for the transgressors" (Isa. 53:12).

Christ began His work as intercessor during

His life on earth. Think of the high-priestly prayer on behalf of His disciples and of all who should, through them, believe in His name. Think of His words to Peter, "I have prayed for you, that your faith may not fail" (Luke 22:32). These words are proof of how intensely personal His intercession is. And on the cross He spoke as intercessor too, "Father, forgive them" (Luke 23:34).

Now that Christ is seated at God's right hand, He continues the work of intercession without ceasing, as our great High Priest, but the difference now is that He gives His people power to take part in it. Seven times in His farewell discourse to the disciples He repeated the assurance that what they asked for, He would do.

The power of heaven was to be at their disposal. The grace and power of God waited for man's bidding. Through the leading of the Holy Spirit they would know what the will of God was. They would learn in faith to pray in His name.

He would present their petition to the Father, and through His and their united intercession, the church would be clothed with the power of the Spirit.

Blessed Redeemer,

What wonderful grace that You call us to share in Your intercession! Stir up in us a consciousness of the glory of our calling, and of all the rich blessing which Your church, through intercession in Your name, can bring down upon this earth.

May Your Holy Spirit work in Your people a deep conviction of the sin of restraining prayer, of the sloth and unbelief and selfishness that is the cause of it, and of Your loving desire to pour out the Spirit of prayer in answer to their petitions – for Your name's sake.

Amen.

Stand in the gap

Jesus Christ, the great Intercessor,
continues to pray for us.

CHAPTER 7

The Intercessors
God Seeks

I have posted watchmen on your walls, O Jerusalem;
they will never be silent day or night. You who call
on the Lord, give yourselves no rest.

~ Isaiah 62:6 ~

Watchmen are usually placed on the walls of a city
to warn the rulers of coming danger. God appoints
watchmen not only to warn people – often they will
not hear – but also so they can summon Him to
come to their aid whenever need or enemy may be
threatening. The great mark of intercessors is that
they are not to hold their peace day or night, not to

rest, and to give God no rest, until the deliverance comes. In faith they may count upon the assurance that God will answer their prayers.

It is of this that our Lord Jesus said, "Will not God bring about justice for His chosen ones, who cry out to Him day and night?" (Luke 18:7). From every land the voice is heard that the church of Christ, under the influence of the power of the world and the earthly mindedness it brings, is losing its influence over its members.

There is but little proof of God's presence in the conversion of sinners or the holiness of His people. With most Christians there is a complete neglect of Christ's call to do their part in the extension of His kingdom. The power of the Holy Spirit is hardly felt or experienced.

Amid all the discussions of what can be done to attract young and old to the study of God's Word or to awaken love for the services of His house, one hears little of the indispensable necessity of the power of the Holy Spirit in the ministry and the membership of the church.

One sees little sign of the conviction and confession that, because of the lack of prayer, the workings of the Spirit are feeble. It is only by united, fervent prayer that change can be brought about. If ever there was a time when God's elect should cry day and night to Him, it is now.

Won't you offer yourself to God for this blessed

task of intercession and learn to count it as the highest privilege of your life that you can be a channel through which God's blessing can be brought down to earth?

Ever Blessed Father,

Raise up intercessors that would please You. We ask that You give us men and women to act as Your remembrances – taking no rest and giving You no rest, until Your church again becomes a praise in the earth.

Blessed Father, let Your Spirit teach us how to pray.

Amen.

Stand in the gap

Let God use you as a channel through which His blessings can be brought down to earth.

CHAPTER 8

The School of Intercession

During the days of Jesus' life on earth, He offered up prayers and petitions with loud cries and tears ... and He was heard because of His reverent submission.

~ Hebrews 5:7 ~

Christ, as Head, is Intercessor in heaven; we, as members of His body, are partners with Him on earth. Let no one imagine that it cost Christ nothing to become an intercessor. He could not without this be our example. What do we read of Him? "Though the LORD makes His life a guilt offering, He will see His offspring ... The suffering of His soul ... therefore will I give Him a portion among the great ... because He poured out His life unto death ... " (Isa. 53:10-12). Notice that the expression in regard to the pouring out of His life is repeated three times.

The pouring out of the life – that is the divine meaning of intercession. Nothing less than this was needed if His sacrifice and prayer were to have power with God. This giving of Himself over to live and die to save the perishing, was a revelation of the spirit that has the power to prevail with God.

If we as helpers and fellow-laborers with the Lord Jesus are to share His power of intercession, we also need to experience the suffering of soul that Jesus experienced, the giving up of our lives and its pleasures for the one supreme work of interceding for our fellowman.

Intercession should not be just a passing interest. It must become an ever-growing object of intense desire for which, above everything, we long and live. It is the life of consecration and self-sacrifice that will indeed give power to intercession (Acts 15:26; 20:24; Phil. 2:17; Rev. 12:11).

The longer we study this blessed truth and think of what it means to exercise this power for the glory of God and the salvation of people, the deeper our conviction will become that it is worth giving up everything to take part with Christ in His work of intercession.

Blessed Lord Jesus,

Teach us how to unite with You in calling upon God for the souls You have bought.

Let Your love fill us and all Your saints that we may learn to plead for the power of Your Holy Spirit to be made known.

Amen.

Stand in the gap

You are to give up your life and
its pleasures for the supreme work
of interceding for others.

CHAPTER 9

The Power in the Name of Jesus

> *"Until now you have not asked for anything in My name. Ask and you will receive, and your joy will be complete. In that day you will ask in My name."*
>
> ~ *John 16:24, 26* ~

During Christ's life on earth the disciples knew but little of the power of prayer. In Gethsemane especially, Peter and the others failed miserably. They had no concept of what it was to ask in the name of Jesus and to receive.

The Lord promised them that in that day which was coming, they would be able to pray with such a power in His name that they might ask for anything and it would be given to them.

"Until now you have not asked for anything in My name. Ask and you will receive, and your joy will be complete" (John 16:24). "In that day you will ask in My name" (John 16:26). Therefore you will receive.

These two conditions are still found in the church. With the great majority of Christians there is such a lack of knowledge of their oneness with Christ Jesus, and of the Holy Spirit as the Spirit of prayer, that they do not even try to claim the wonderful promises Christ gives here. But where God's children know what it is to abide in Christ, in vital union with Him and to yield to the Holy Spirit's teaching, they begin to learn that their intercession accomplishes much. God will give the power of His Spirit in answer to their prayers.

It is faith in the power of Jesus' name, and in our right to use it that will give us the courage to follow on when God invites us to the holy office of intercessor. When our Lord Jesus, in His farewell discourse, gave His unlimited prayer promise, He sent the disciples out into the world with this knowledge, "He who sits upon the throne and lives in my heart, has promised that I will receive what I ask in His name. He will do it."

If we only knew what it is to yield ourselves absolutely to Jesus Christ and His service, how our eyes would be opened to see that intense and unceasing prayerfulness is the essential mark of a healthy spiritual life.

The power of all-prevailing intercession will indeed be the portion of those who live only in and for their Lord!

Blessed Savior,

Give us the grace of the Holy Spirit so that we might live in You, and with You, and for You. Allow us to boldly look to You for the assurance that our prayers are heard.

Amen.

Stand in the gap

Faith in the power of Jesus' name gives us courage as intercessors.

CHAPTER 10

Prayer, the Work of the Spirit

God sent the Spirit of His Son into our hearts, the Spirit who calls out, "Abba, Father."

~ Galatians 4:6 ~

We know what "Abba, Father" meant in the mouth of Christ in Gethsemane. It was the entire surrender of Himself to death that the holy will of God's love in redemption of sinners might be accomplished. In His prayer He was ready for any sacrifice, even to the yielding of His life.

In that prayer the heart of Him whose place is at the right hand of God is revealed to us, with the wonderful power of intercession that He exercises and the power to pour down the Holy Spirit.

The Holy Spirit has been bestowed by the Father to breathe the very Spirit of His Son into our hearts. Our Lord wants us to yield ourselves as wholly to God as He did; to pray like Him, that God's will of love should be done on earth at any cost.

As God's love is revealed in His desire for the salvation of souls, Jesus' desire was made plain when He gave Himself for them. And He now asks of His people to be filled by that same love, so that they can give themselves wholly to the work of intercession and, at any cost, pray down God's love upon the perishing.

And if anyone should think that this is too high and beyond their reach, the Holy Spirit is actually given into our hearts so that we may pray as Jesus did in His power and in His name.

It is the man who yields himself wholly to the leading of the Holy Spirit who will feel urged, by the compulsion of a divine love, to live a life of continual intercession because he knows that God is working in him.

Now we can understand how Christ could give such unlimited promises of answer to prayer to His disciples; they first had to be filled with the Holy Spirit. Now we understand how God can give such a high place to intercession in the fulfillment of His purpose of redemption. It is the Holy Spirit who breathes God's own desire into us and enables us to intercede for souls.

Abba Father,

May Your Holy Spirit help us to intercede unceasingly in love for the souls Christ died for.

Give to Your children the vision of the blessedness and the power that come to those who yield themselves to this high calling.

Amen.

Stand in the gap

Be filled with the Holy Spirit
and pray in love.

CHAPTER 11

Christ, Our Example in Intercession

He will divide the spoils with the strong, because ...
He bore the sin of many, and made intercession for
the transgressors.

~ *Isaiah 53:12* ~

Christ "made intercession for the transgressors."
What did that mean to Him?

Think of what it cost Christ to pray that prayer
effectually. He had to pour out His own soul as an
offering for sin, and cry in Gethsemane, "Father,
may Your will be done" (Matt. 26:42).

Think what moved Him to sacrifice Himself to

the point of death! It was His love for the Father – that His holiness might be manifested. It was also His love for souls – that they might be partakers of His holiness.

Just consider the reward He won! As Conqueror of every enemy, Christ is seated at the right hand of God with the power of unlimited and assured intercession. And He would see His seed, a generation of those of the same mind as Himself, whom He could train to share in His great work of intercession.

And what does this mean for us, when we also seek to pray for the transgressors? That we, too, yield ourselves wholly to the glory of the holiness and the love of the Father. Therefore we can also say, Your will be done God, whatever the cost, we too sacrifice ourselves, even to the pouring out of our souls unto death.

The Lord Jesus has in His very act taken us up into a partnership with Himself to carry out the great work of intercession. He in heaven and we on earth must be of one mind – we must have only one aim in life.

That aim is that we should love the Father, as well as the lost, by dedicating our lives to intercession for God's blessing. The burning desire of Father and Son for the salvation of souls must be the burning desire of our hearts too.

What an honor! What a blessing! And what power we have to do the work because He lives, and by His

Spirit He pours forth His love into our hearts!

Everlasting God of Love,

Open our eyes to the vision of the glory of Your Son, as He ever lives to pray.

Open our eyes to the glory of the grace that enables us, in His likeness, to pray for the transgressors, for Jesus' sake.

Amen.

Stand in the gap

Let the salvation of souls be the
burning desire of your heart.

CHAPTER 12

God's Will and Ours

"Your will be done."

~ *Matthew 26:42* ~

It is God's prerogative that everything in heaven and earth is to be done according to His will and as the fulfillment of His desires. When He made man in His image it was, above all, that his desires were to be in perfect accord with the desires of God. This is the high honor of being in the likeness of God. We are to feel and wish just as God does. Man was to be the embodiment and fulfillment of God's desires.

When God created man with the power of free will and choice, He limited Himself in the exercise of His will. And when man had fallen and yielded himself to the will of God's enemy, God in His infinite love set about the great work of winning man back to make the desires of God his own.

As in God, so in man, desire is the great moving power. And just as man had yielded himself to a life of desire after the things of the earth and the flesh, God had to redeem him and educate him into a life of harmony with Himself. His one aim was that man's desire should be in perfect harmony with His own.

The biggest step towards achieving this aim was when the Son of the Father came into this world to reproduce the divine desires in His human nature, and in His prayer to yield Himself to the perfect fulfillment of all that God wished and willed.

The Son, as man, said in agony and blood, "Your will be done," and surrendered even to being forsaken by God. He did this so that the power that had deceived man might be conquered and deliverance won. It was in this wonderful and complete harmony between the Father and the Son when the Son said, "Your will be done," that the great redemption was accomplished.

And now the great work of attaining that redemption is this: believers have to say, firstly for themselves and then in lives devoted to intercession for others, "Your will be done on earth as it is in heaven" (Matt. 6:10). As we plead for the church – its ministers and its missionaries, its strong Christians or its young converts – for the unsaved, whether nominally Christian or unconverted, we have the privilege of knowing that we are pleading for what God wills, and that through our prayers His will is to be done on earth as it is in heaven.

Lord Jesus,

Help us not to limit You through lack of prayer. Grant us the desire to pray for Your will to be done in all situations.

Let us feel the burden of all those unsaved souls heavily on our hearts so we will pray that much harder for their salvation.

Amen.

Stand in the gap

Know that your prayers for the church and the unsaved are what God wills.

Chapter 13

The Blessedness of a Life of Intercession

Then hear from heaven their prayer and their plea, and uphold their cause.

~ 2 Chronicles 6:35 ~

What an unspeakable grace to be allowed to deal with God in intercession for the supply of other's needs! To be able to take part in Christ's great work as Intercessor is such a blessing. It is wonderful to be in close union with Him and to mingle your prayers with His! What an honor to have power with God in heaven over souls and to obtain for them what they do not even know or think!

What a privilege, as a steward of the grace of God, to bring to Him the state of the church or individual souls, of ministers of the Word, or of missionaries in far away lands, and plead on their behalf until He entrusts you with the answer!

What a blessing, to strive together in prayer with other believers until the victory is gained here on earth or over the powers of darkness in high places!

It is indeed worth living for to know that God will use you as an intercessor to receive and dispense His heavenly blessing and, above all, the power of His Holy Spirit here on earth.

This is in its very act the life of heaven, the life of the Lord Jesus Himself in His self-denying love, taking possession of you and urging you to yield yourself wholly to bear the burden of souls before Him and to plead that they may live.

Too long have we thought of prayer simply as a means for the supplying of our needs in life and service. May God help us to see the place intercession takes in His divine counsel and in His work for the kingdom.

May our hearts indeed feel that there is no honor or blessing on earth equal to the privilege of waiting upon God and bringing down from heaven and of opening the way on earth for the blessing He delights to give!

Father,

Let Your life flow down to this earth, and fill the hearts of Your children! As the Lord Jesus pours out His love in His unceasing intercession in heaven, let us also live such a life on earth, a life of overflowing love and never-ending intercession.

Amen.

Stand in the gap

God wants to use you to dispense His heavenly blessings and the power of the Holy Spirit on earth.

CHAPTER 14

The Place of Prayer

They all joined together constantly in prayer.

~ Acts 1:14 ~

The last words that Christ spoke before He left this earth give us the four great notes of His church, "Wait for the gift My Father promised" (Acts 1:4), "You will receive power when the Holy Spirit comes on you; ... and you will be My witnesses in Jerusalem ... and to the ends of the earth" (Acts 1:8).

United and unceasing prayer, the power of the Holy Spirit, living witnesses to the living Christ, from Jerusalem to the ends of the earth – these are the marks of the true gospel, of the true ministry, of the true church of the New Testament.

A church of united and unceasing prayerfulness, a ministry filled with the Holy Spirit, members acting as living witnesses to a living Christ with a message to every creature on earth – this was the church that Christ founded, this was the church that went out to conquer the world.

When Christ had ascended to heaven, the disciples knew at once what their work was to be: continuing to pray together constantly. They were to be bound together by the love and Spirit of Christ into one body. It was this that gave them their wonderful power in heaven with God and upon earth with men.

Their one duty was to wait in united and unceasing prayer for the power of the Holy Spirit as the power from on high for their witness to Christ to the ends of the earth. A praying church, a Spirit-filled church, a witnessing church, with all the world as its sphere and aim – this is the church of Jesus Christ.

As long as it maintained this character it had power to conquer. But unfortunately, as it came under the influence of the world, it lost its heavenly, supernatural beauty and strength! The church became unfaithful in prayer, feeble in the workings of the Spirit, formal in its witnessing to Christ, and unfaithful to its worldwide mission!

Blessed Lord Jesus,

Have mercy upon Your church, and give her the Spirit of prayer and supplication as of old, that Your church may prove and testify of Your power that rests upon her, to win the world to Your feet.

Amen.

Stand in the gap

Pray for the church, for united and unceasing prayerfulness.

CHAPTER 15

Paul as an Intercessor

I kneel before the Father ... that out of His glorious riches He may strengthen you with power through His Spirit.

~ Ephesians 3:14, 16 ~

We think of Paul as the great missionary, the great preacher, the great writer, the great apostle "in labors more abundant ..." (2 Cor. 11:23 KJV). We do not think of him as the intercessor who sought and obtained, through prayer, the power that rested upon all his other activities, and brought down the blessing that rested on the churches that he served.

In our verse for today we read what Paul wrote

to the Ephesians. Think of what he said to the Thessalonians, "Night and day we pray most earnestly that we may ... supply what is lacking in your faith ... May He strengthen your hearts so that you will be blameless and holy ..." (1 Thess. 3:10, 13 KJV). To the Romans, "I remember you in my prayers at all times" (Rom. 1:9-10 KJV). To the Philippians, "In all my prayers for all of you, I always pray with joy" (Phil. 1:4). And to the Colossians, "We have not stopped praying for you ... I want you to know how much I am struggling for you" (Col. 1:9; 2:1).

Day and night he cried to God in his intercession for them, that the light and the power of the Holy Spirit might be in them. As earnestly as he believed in the power of his intercession for them so also did he believe in the blessing that theirs would bring upon him. "I urge you ... to join me in my struggle by praying to God for me" (Rom. 15:30). "[God] will deliver us ... as you help us by your prayers" (2 Cor. 1:10-11). "Pray also for me, that whenever I open my mouth, words may be given me so that I will fearlessly make known the mystery of the gospel" (Eph. 6:19). "Through your prayers ... what has happened to me will turn out for my deliverance" (Phil. 1:19).

The whole relationship between a pastor and the congregation depends on united continual prayerfulness. Their whole relationship to each other is a heavenly one, spiritual and divine, and can only be maintained by unceasing prayer.

It is when ministers and people wake up and are conscious of the fact that the power and blessing of the Holy Spirit is waiting for their united and unceasing prayer that the church will begin to know something of what apostolic Christianity is.

Ever Blessed Father,

We humbly ask You to once again restore the spirit of supplication and intercession to Your church, for Jesus' sake.

Amen.

Stand in the gap

The power and blessing of the Holy Spirit in the church depends on united and unceasing prayer.

CHAPTER 16

Intercession for Laborers

> *"The harvest is plentiful but the workers are few. Ask the Lord of the harvest, therefore, to send out workers into His harvest field."*
>
> ~ *Matthew 9:37-38* ~

The disciples understood very little of what these words meant. Christ gave them as a seed-thought to be lodged in their hearts for later use.

At Pentecost, when they saw how many of the new converts were ready in the power of the Spirit to testify about Christ, they must have felt how the ten days of continuous, united prayer had brought this blessing. This is an example of the fruit of the Spirit's power – laborers in the harvest.

Christ meant to teach us that however large the field may be and however few the laborers, prayer is the best, the surest, and the only means for supplying the need.

What we have to understand is that it is not only in times of need that the prayer must be sent up, but that the whole work is to be carried on in the spirit of prayer. In this way the prayer for workers shall be in perfect harmony with the whole of our lives and efforts.

In the China Inland Mission, when the number of missionaries had gone up to two hundred, at a conference held in China they felt so deeply the need for more laborers for the districts that were unprovided for that, after much prayer, they felt at liberty to ask God to give them one hundred additional laborers and ten thousand pounds to meet expenses, all within a year.

They agreed to continue in prayer every day throughout the year. At the end of a year, the one hundred suitable men and women had been found with eleven thousand pounds.

Churches all complain about the lack of workers and funds to meet the needs of the world, its open fields, and its waiting souls.

Yet Christ's voice calls us to the united and unceasing prayer of the first disciples. God is faithful, by the power of His Spirit, to supply every need.

Let the church unite in prayer and supplication. God hears prayer.

Blessed Lord Jesus,

Teach Your church what it means to live and labor for You in the Spirit of unceasing prayerfulness, that our faith may rise to the assurance that You will meet the crying need of a dying world in a way that surpasses all expectations.

Amen.

Stand in the gap

God hears prayers and is faithful
to supply every need.

Chapter 17

Intercession for Individual Souls

You, O Israelites, will be gathered up one by one.

~ Isaiah 27:12 ~

In our body every member has its appointed place. This is also true in society and in the church. The work must always aim at the welfare and the highest perfection of the whole through the cooperation of every individual member.

In the church many believe that the salvation of people is the minister's job, whereas he generally only deals with the crowd as a whole and seldom reaches the individual.

This is the cause of a twofold evil. The individual believer does not understand that it is necessary for him to testify to those around him – not just to save a soul but also for the nourishment and the strengthening of his own spiritual life.

Lost souls suffer an indescribable loss because Christ is not personally brought to them by believers they meet. The thought of intercession for those around us is not a frequent one. How much it would mean to the church and its missions if the act of intercession was restored to its rightful place among believers!

When will Christians learn that God in heaven needs prayer on earth in order to do what He desires? It is when we realize this that we will see that intercession is the chief element in the salvation of souls. All of our efforts are in vain without the power of the Holy Spirit that is given to us in answer to prayer. It is when ministers and people unite in a covenant of prayer and testimony that the church will flourish and that every believer will understand the part he has to take.

What can we do to stir up the spirit of intercession? Firstly, let every Christian, as he begins to get an insight into the need and the power of intercession, begin by exercising it on behalf of single individuals. Pray for your children, your relatives and friends, all whom God brings you into contact with.

If you feel that you do not have the power to intercede, let the discovery humble you and drive you to the mercy seat. God wants every child of His to intercede for the perishing. It is the vital breath of the normal Christian life – the proof that it is born from above.

Then pray intensely and persistently for God to give you the power of His Holy Spirit, that the power of intercession may have the place that God will honor.

Father God,

Thank You for giving me the ability to intercede for others. Let me pray wisely and persistently, day and night.

Amen.

Stand in the gap

God in heaven needs prayer on earth to do what He desires.

CHAPTER 18

Intercession for Ministers

Pray also for me.

~ Ephesians 6:19 ~

Pray for us, too.

~ Colossians 4:3 ~

Finally, brothers, pray for us.

~ 2 Thessalonians 3:1 ~

These expressions of Paul suggest how strong his conviction must have been that Christians have power with God and their prayers can bring new strength. He had such a sense of the actual unity of the body of Christ. He saw unity in the interdependence of each member, even the most honorable, and on the life that flowed through the whole body.

This encouraged him to rouse Christians, for their own sakes and for his sake and for the sake of the kingdom of God, with his call, "Devote yourselves to prayer, being watchful and thankful. And pray for us, too" (Col. 4:2-3).

The church depends upon the ministry more than we realize. The place of the minister is so high, as the steward of the mysteries of God and as the ambassador for God, that unfaithfulness or inefficiency severely weakens his church.

If Paul, after having preached for twenty years in the power of God, still needed the prayer of the church, how much more does the ministry in our day need it?

The minister needs the prayer of his people. He has a right to it. In fact, he is dependent on it. It is his task to train Christians for their work of intercession on behalf of the church and the world. He must begin with training them to pray for himself. He may have to begin even further back and learn to pray more for himself and for them. Let all intercessors who are seeking to enter more deeply into their blessed work give a larger place to the ministry, whether of their own church or of other churches.

Let them plead with God for individual men and for special circles. Let them continue in prayer so that ministers may be men of power, men of prayer, and men full of the Holy Spirit. Pray for the ministry!

Our Father in heaven,

We humbly pray for You to awaken believers to a sense of their calling to pray for the ministers of the gospel in the spirit of faith.

Amen.

Stand in the gap

Pray for ministers,
that they be men of power,
prayer and full of the Holy Spirit.

CHAPTER 19

Prayer for All Saints

Pray in the Spirit on all occasions with all kinds of prayers and requests. With this in mind, be alert and always keep on praying for all the saints.

~ Ephesians 6:18 ~

Notice how Paul repeats the words in the intensity of his desire to reach the hearts of his readers. "Pray on *all* occasions with *all* prayers and requests." That is *"all* occasions, *all* prayers, *all* requests." The words claim thought, if they are to meet with the needed response.

Paul felt so deeply the unity of the body of Christ, and he was so sure that the unity could only be realized in the exercise of love and prayer.

Therefore, he pleaded with the believers at Ephesus to pray for all saints unceasingly and fervently, not only in their immediate circle, but for all in the church of Christ of whom they might hear. "Unity is strength."

As we exercise this power of intercession with perseverance, we shall be delivered from self with all its feeble prayers and lifted up to that enlargement of heart in which the love of Christ can flow freely and fully through us.

The great lack in true believers is often that they are occupied with themselves and with what God must do for them in their prayers. Let us realize that here is a call to every believer to give himself to the exercise of love and prayer without ceasing.

When we forget ourselves, having faith that God will take charge of us, and yield ourselves to calling down the blessing of God upon our fellow believers – then the whole church will be fitted to do its work of making Christ known to every creature. This is the healthy and blessed life of someone who has yielded himself wholly to Christ Jesus.

Pray for God's children and the church around you. Pray for all the work they are or should be doing. Pray at all times in the Spirit for all of God's saints.

There is no blessing greater than that of constant communion with God. There is no way that leads to the enjoyment of this more surely than the life of intercession for which these words of Paul appeal so pleadingly.

Heavenly Father,

Help me not to be so selfish in my prayers. I pray that You will enlarge the parameter of my prayers so that I am no longer self-focused but am consumed by the needs of others too.

Amen.

Stand in the gap

Give yourself to the exercise of love
and prayer without ceasing.

CHAPTER 20

Missionary Intercession

> *After they had fasted and prayed, they placed their hands on them and sent them off.*
>
> ~ *Acts 13:3* ~

The supreme question of foreign missions is how to multiply the number of Christians who will individually and collectively wield this force of intercession so that souls can be saved. Every other consideration and plan is secondary to that of using the forces of prayer.

We take for granted that those who love this work, and bear it upon their hearts, will follow the scriptural command to pray unceasingly for its triumph.

These people display an attitude of intercession at all times and during all seasons. They refuse to let go of God until He has crowned His workers with victory.

Missions have their root in the love of Christ, which was proven on the cross and now lives in our hearts. As men are so earnest in seeking to carry out God's plans for the natural world, so God's children should be as wholehearted in seeking to bring Christ's love to all mankind. Intercession is the chief means appointed by God to bring the great redemption within the reach of all.

Pray for missionaries, that the Christ-life may be clear and strong. Pray also that they may be people of prayer and filled with love, in whom the power of the spiritual life is made manifest.

Pray for Christians, that they may know the glory of the mystery among the unsaved so that with Christ in them they will know the hope of glory. Pray for baptism classes and all the pupils in schools, that the teaching of God's Word may be in power.

Pray especially for pastors and evangelists, that the Holy Spirit may fill them to be witnesses for Christ among their fellow-citizens.

Pray, above all, for the church of Christ, that it may be lifted out of its indifference and that every believer may be brought to understand that the one object of his life is to help to make Christ King on the earth.

Our Gracious God,

Our eyes are on You. Be merciful, hear our prayers, and by the Holy Spirit reveal the presence and the power of Christ in the work of Your servants.

Amen.

Stand in the gap

Intercession is the chief means appointed by God to bring the great redemption within the reach of all.

CHAPTER 21

The Grace of Intercession

Devote yourselves to prayer, being watchful and thankful. Pray for us, too.

~ Colossians 4:2-3 ~

Nothing can bring us nearer to God, or lead us deeper into His love, than the work of intercession. Nothing can give us a higher experience of the likeness of God than the power of pouring out our hearts to God in prayer for people around us.

Nothing can so closely link us to Jesus Christ, the great Intercessor, and give us the experience of His power and Spirit resting on us than the yielding of our lives to the work of bringing others to Christ.

Nothing can show us more of the powerful working of the Holy Spirit than the prayer breathed by Him into our hearts, "Abba, Father," in all the fullness of meaning that it had for Christ in Gethsemane.

Nothing can so help us prove the power and the faithfulness of God to His Word than when we reach out in intercession to the multitudes. We pour out our souls as a living sacrifice before God. Our one persistent prayer is that He open the windows of heaven and send down His abundant blessing. God will be glorified, our souls will reach their highest destiny, and God's kingdom will come.

Nothing will help us understand and experience the living unity of the body of Christ and its irresistible power than the daily and continued fellowship with God's children. His children stand together in the persistent plea that God will arise and have mercy upon Zion and make her a light and a life to those who are sitting in darkness.

If only we could see what we are losing by not living in fervent intercession! What could we possibly lose for ourselves and for the world if we allow God's Spirit, as a Spirit of grace and of supplication, to master our whole being?

In heaven Christ lives to pray. His whole communion with His Father is prayer – an asking and receiving of the fullness of the Spirit for His people. God delights in nothing so much as in our prayers. We must start to believe that the highest blessings of heaven will unfold before us when we pray more.

Blessed Father,

Pour down the Spirit of supplication and intercession on Your people, for Jesus Christ's sake.

Amen.

Stand in the gap

Let the work of intercession draw you nearer to God and others.

CHAPTER 22

United Intercession

There is one body and one Spirit.

~ Ephesians 4:4 ~

Every part of the physical body needs to do its own share in order for the whole body to be strong and healthy. So it is in the body of Christ too. There are, unfortunately, too many people who look upon salvation only in connection with their own happiness.

There are some people, though, who truly seek in prayer and work to bring others to share in their happiness; however, they do not yet understand that they have a calling to enlarge their hearts to take the whole body of Christ Jesus into their love and their intercession – and not just their friends or their church.

Yet this is what the Spirit and the love of Christ will enable them to do. It is only when intercession for the whole church, by the whole church, ascends to God's throne that the Spirit of unity and power can have its full sway.

The desire that has been awakened for closer union between the different branches of the church of Christ is a reason for thanksgiving. But the difficulties are great and, in the case of different nationalities of the world, so apparently inseparable that the thought of a united church on earth appears beyond reach.

Let us bless God that there is a unity that can be found in Christ Jesus that is deeper and stronger than any visible separation. There is a way in which even now, amidst all diversity, that the unity can be exemplified and utilized to increase divine strength and blessing in the work of the kingdom. It is in the cultivation and increase of the Spirit and in the exercise of intercession that true unity can be realized.

As believers are taught what the meaning of their calling as a royal priesthood is, they are led to see that God is not confined in His love or promises to their limited spheres of labor. God invites them to enlarge their hearts and like Christ – we may say like Paul too – to pray for all who believe, or can yet be brought to believe, that this earth and the church of Christ in it will, by intercession, be bound to the throne of heaven as it has never yet been.

Let Christians and ministers agree and bind themselves together for this worldwide intercession. It will strengthen the confidence that prayer will be heard and that their prayers too will become indispensable for the coming of the Kingdom.

Heavenly Father,

May we unite and bind ourselves together as one as we pray necessary and indispensable prayers of intercession.

Amen.

Stand in the gap

It is only when intercession for the whole church, by the whole church, ascends to God's throne that the Spirit of unity and power can have its full sway.

CHAPTER 23

Unceasing Intercession

> *Pray continually.*
>
> *~ 1 Thessalonians 5:17 ~*

There is a marked difference between the average Christian's life of service to God and the standard set in Scripture. The average Christian's chief concern is grace to pardon our sins and to live life in such a way so as to secure our entrance into heaven.

The biblical standard is so much higher – a Christian surrendering himself with all his powers, with his time and thought and love wholly yielded to the glorious God who has redeemed him, whom he now delights in serving, in whose fellowship is heaven begun.

To the average Christian the command to "Pray continually" is simply a needless and impossible life of perfection. Who can do it? We can get to heaven without it. Yet to the true believer it holds out the promise of the highest happiness, of a life crowned by all the blessings that can be brought down on souls through intercession. And as he perseveres, it becomes increasingly his highest aim upon earth, his highest joy, his highest experience of the wonderful fellowship with the holy God.

"Pray continually!" Let us take that word in a large faith, as a promise of what God's Spirit will work in us, of how close and intimate our union to the Lord Jesus can be, and of our likeness to Him, in His ever-blessed intercession at the right hand of God.

Let it become to us one of the chief elements of our heavenly calling to be the stewards and administrators of God's grace to the world around us. As we think of how Christ said, "I in them and You in Me" (John 17:23), let us believe that just as the Father worked in Him, so Christ, the interceding High Priest, will work and pray in us.

As the faith of our high calling fills our hearts we shall begin literally to feel that there is nothing on earth that can be compared with the privilege of being God's priests.

This privilege includes walking continuously in His holy presence, bringing the burden of the souls around us to the foot of His throne, and receiving at His hands the power and blessing to share with our fellow man.

This is indeed the fulfillment of the Word of old, which said that man was created in the likeness and the image of God (Gen. 1:27).

Father God,

May I pray continually in faith and intercession. Grant that I may realize that nothing compares to doing Your work.

Amen.

Stand in the gap

Let continual intercession
be your highest aim, joy and
experience of wonderful fellowship
with the holy God.

CHAPTER 24

Intercession, the Link between Heaven and Earth

"Your will be done on earth as it is in heaven."

~ Matthew 6:10 ~

When God created heaven and earth, He meant heaven to be the divine pattern to which earth was to be conformed; "on earth as it is in heaven" was to be the law of its existence.

This truth calls us to think of what constitutes the glory of heaven. God is all in all there. Everything lives in Him and to His glory.

We then think of what this earth has now become with all its sin and misery. Here on earth the majority of people are without any knowledge of the true God, and those who do know Him are, for the most part, utterly indifferent to His claims and estranged from His holiness and love. What a revolution, what a miracle is needed if the word is to be fulfilled, "on earth as it is in heaven."

How is this word ever to come true? Through the prayers of God's children. Our Lord teaches us to pray for it. Intercession is to be the great link between heaven and earth.

The intercession of the Son that was begun on earth, continued in heaven, and is carried on by His redeemed people upon earth, will bring about the mighty change, "on earth as it is in heaven." As Christ said, "I have come to do Your will" (Heb. 10:9), until He prayed the great prayer in Gethsemane, "May Your will be done" (Matt. 26:42).

So His redeemed ones, those who yield themselves fully to His mind and Spirit, make His prayer their own and continually send up the cry, "May Your will be done on earth as it is in heaven."

Every prayer of a parent for a child, of a believer for the saving of the lost, or for more grace to those who have been saved, is part of the great unceasing cry going up day and night from this earth, "On earth as it is in heaven."

But it is when God's children not only learn

to pray for their immediate circles and interests but also enlarge their hearts to take in the whole church and the whole world, that their united supplication will have power with God. Then the day will advance when it shall indeed be "on earth as it is in heaven" – the whole earth will be filled with the glory of God.

Child of God, will you not yield yourself, like Christ, to live with this one prayer, "Father ... Your will be done, on earth as it is in heaven"?

"Our Father in Heaven,

Hallowed be Your name, Your kingdom come, Your will be done on earth as it is in heaven."

Amen (Luke 11:2).

Stand in the gap

Intercession is the great link between heaven and earth.

CHAPTER 25

The Fulfillment of God's Desires

> *For the LORD has chosen Zion ... for His dwelling ...*
> *"this is My resting place ... for I have desired it."*
> ~ Psalm 132:13-14 ~

In this Scripture passage you have the one great desire of God that moved Him in the work of redemption. His heart longs for man to dwell with Him and Him in man.

To Moses He said, "Have them make a sanctuary for Me, and I will dwell among them" (Exod. 25:8). Just as Israel had to prepare the dwelling for God, so now are His children called to yield themselves to God so He can dwell in them and to win others to become His habitation. As the desire of God towards us fills the heart, it will awaken within us the desire to gather others around us to become His dwelling too.

What an honor! What a high calling to count worldly business as entirely secondary and to find life and delight in winning souls in whom God may find His heart's delight! "Here is My resting place ... for I have desired it."

And this is what I can do through intercession. I can pray for God to give His Holy Spirit to those around me. It is God's great plan that man shall build Him a dwelling place. It is in answer to the unceasing intercession of His children that God will give His power and blessing. As this great desire of God fills us, we shall give ourselves wholly to labor for its fulfillment.

Think of David when he thought of God's desire to dwell in Israel, how he said, "I will allow no sleep to my eyes, no slumber to my eyelids, till I find a place for the LORD, a dwelling for the Mighty One of Jacob" (Ps. 132:4-5). And will we not, to whom it has been revealed what that indwelling of God may be, give our lives for the fulfillment of His heart's desire?

Let us begin, as never before, to pray for our children, for the souls around us, and for all the world. Not only because we love them, but because

God longs for them and gives us the honor of being the channels through whom His blessing is brought down.

Child of God, awake to the realization of what it means that God is seeking to train you as an intercessor so the great desire of His loving heart can be satisfied!

O God,

Who has said of human hearts, "Here is My resting place ... for I have desired it," teach us to pray, day and night, that the desire of Your heart may be fulfilled.

Amen.

Standing in the gap

Delight in winning souls in whom God may find His heart's delight.

CHAPTER 26

The Fulfillment of Man's Desires

Delight yourself in the LORD and He will give you the desires of your heart.

~ Psalm 37:4 ~

God is love; an ever-flowing fountain out of which streams the unceasing desire to make His creatures the partakers of all the holiness and the blessedness there is in Himself. This desire for the salvation of souls is God's perfect will, His highest glory.

God's loving desire to get His place in the heart of people, is imparted to all His children who are willing to yield themselves wholly to Him. It is in

this that the likeness and image of God consist –
to have a heart in which His love takes complete
possession and leads us to find our highest joy in
loving as He does.

It is thus that our verse finds its fulfillment,
"Delight yourself in the LORD," and in His life of love,
"and He will give you the desires of your heart."
Count on it that the intercession of love, rising up
to heaven, will be met with the fulfillment of the
desire of our hearts.

We may be sure that, as we delight in what
God delights in, such prayer is inspired by God
and will have its answer. And our prayer becomes
unceasingly, "Your desires, Father, are mine. Your
holy will of love is my will too."

In fellowship with Him we get the courage, with
our whole will and strength, to bring people before
His throne with an ever-growing confidence that
our prayers will be heard.

As we reach out in love, we will have the power
to take hold of the will of God to bless and to believe
that God will work out His own blessed will in
giving us the desire of our hearts. He will do this
because the fulfillment of His desire has been the
delight of our souls.

We then become, in the highest sense of the
word, God's fellow-laborers. Our prayer becomes
part of God's divine work of reaching and saving the
lost. And we learn to find our happiness in losing

ourselves in the salvation of those around us.

Father,

Teach us that nothing less than delighting ourselves in You, and in Your desires toward people, can inspire us to pray unceasingly, and give us the assurance of an answer.

Amen.

Stand in the gap

Let the desire of your heart
be the salvation of souls.

CHAPTER 27

My Great Desire

One thing I ask of the LORD, this is what I seek: that I may dwell in the house of the LORD all the days of my life, to gaze upon the beauty of the LORD and to seek Him in His temple.

~ Psalm 27:4 ~

Here we have man's response to God's desire to live in us. When the desire of God towards us begins to rule the life and heart, our desire is fixed on one thing, and that is to dwell in the house of the Lord all the days of our lives.

Dwelling therefore means to behold the beauty of the Lord, to worship Him in the beauty of holiness, and then to inquire in His temple and learn what it means that God has said, "I the LORD have spoken, and I will do it" (Ezek. 22:14) and "Once again I will yield to the plea of the house of Israel and do this for them" (Ezek. 36:37).

The more we realize that the desire of God's love is to give His rest in the heart, and the more our desire increases to dwell every day in His temple and behold His beauty, the more the Spirit of intercession will grow upon us to claim all that God has promised in His new covenant.

Whether we think of our churches and country, of our homes and schools; whether we think of the saved and all their needs, or the unsaved and their danger, the thought that God is indeed longing to find His home and rest in the hearts of people, if He be only asked, will rouse our whole being to strive for Zion's sake not to hold our peace.

All thoughts of our weakness and unworthiness will be forgotten in the wonderful assurance that He has said of human hearts, "This is My resting place for ever; here I will sit enthroned, for I have desired it" (Ps. 132:14).

Our faith begins to see how high our calling is and how fervent, intense, persistent prayer is necessary for His purpose to be fulfilled. We are then drawn to give up our lives for a closer walk with God. We will wait unceasingly upon Him and will become a testimony to our fellow believers of what God will do in them and in us.

How wonderful that we can have a divine partnership in which God commits the fulfillment of His desires to our keeping! Shame on us that we have so little realized it!

Our Father in Heaven,

We ask You to give, give in power, the Spirit of grace and supplication to Your people, for Jesus' sake.

Amen.

Standing in the gap

Wait unceasingly upon God and be a testimony of what God can do in others.

CHAPTER 28

Intercession Day
and Night

> *"And will not God bring about justice for His chosen
> ones, who cry out to Him day and night? Will He keep
> putting them off?"*
>
> *~ Luke 18:7 ~*

When Nehemiah heard of the destruction of
Jerusalem, he cried to God, "Hear the prayer Your
servant is praying before You day and night" (Neh.
1:6). God said of the watchmen set on the walls of
Jerusalem, "[They] will never be silent day or night"
(Isa. 62:6). And Paul writes, "Night and day we pray
most earnestly ... May He strengthen your hearts so

that you will be blameless and holy in the presence of our God and Father" (1 Thess. 3:10, 13).

Is such prayer night and day really needed and really possible? Yes, when the heart is so entirely consumed by the desire that it cannot rest until this is fulfilled. When life is under the power of the heavenly blessing, then nothing can keep one from sacrificing everything to obtain it.

When a child of God begins to get a real vision into the need of the church and of the world, a vision of the divine redemption which God has promised in the outpouring of love into our hearts, a vision of the power of true intercession to bring down the heavenly blessing, a vision of the honor of being allowed as intercessors to take part in that work, he will regard it as the most heavenly thing on earth to act as intercessor and to cry day and night to God for the revelation of His mighty power.

Let us learn from David, who said, "Zeal for Your house consumes me" (Ps. 69:9). Let us learn from Christ our Lord, of whom these words were so intensely true, that nothing is worth living for more than satisfying the heart of God in His longing for human fellowship and affection and winning hearts to be His dwelling place.

And we also will not give ourselves any rest until we have found place for the Mighty One in our hearts and yielded ourselves to the work of intercession for many whose desire for God is waning.

God grant that our hearts may be so brought under the influence of these divine truths that we may yield ourselves to make our devotion to Christ, and our longing to satisfy the heart of God, the chief object of our lives.

Lord Jesus,

The great Intercessor, who finds in it all Your glory, breath, we pray You, from Your own Spirit into our hearts, for Your name's sake.

Amen.

Stand in the gap

Cry night and day for the revelation
of God's mighty power.

CHAPTER **29**

The High Priest and His Intercession

We do have such a High Priest ... He is able to save completely those who come to God through Him, because He always lives to intercede for them.

~ Hebrews 8:1; 7:25 ~

In Israel, what a difference there was between the high priest and the priests and Levites. The high priest alone had access to the Holy of Holies. He bore on his forehead the golden crown engraved with "Holiness to the Lord," and by his intercession on the great Day of Atonement, he bore the sins of the people.

The priests brought the daily sacrifices and stood before the Lord and came out to bless the people. The difference between the high priest and the priest was great. But still greater was the unity; the priests formed one body with the high priest, sharing with him the power to appear before God to receive and dispense His blessing to His people.

So it is with our great High Priest. He alone has power with God, in a never-ceasing intercession, to obtain from the Father what His people need. And yet, infinite though the distance be between Him and the royal priesthood that surrounds Him for His service, the unity and the fellowship into which His people have been taken up with Him is no less infinite than the apparent diversity.

The blessing that He obtains from His Father for us, He holds for His people to receive from Him through their fervent plea, to be given to the souls among whom He has placed them as His witnesses and representatives.

As long as Christians simply think of being saved, and of a life which will make that salvation secure, they will never understand the mystery of the power of intercession to which they are called.

But when they realize that salvation means a vital life-union with Jesus Christ; an actual sharing of His life dwelling and working in us; and the consecration of our whole being, to live and labor, to think and will, and find our highest joy in living as a royal priesthood; the church will put on her strength and prove, in dealings with God and man, how truly the likeness and the power of Christ dwell in her.

O God,

That You would open our hearts to know and prove what our royal priesthood is – what the real meaning is of our living and praying in the name of Jesus, that what we ask shall indeed be given to us! Lord Jesus, our holy High Priest, breathe the Spirit of Your own holy priesthood into our hearts.

Amen.

Stand in the gap

Pray that the church
will be a royal priesthood,
with Jesus as the
holy High Priest.

CHAPTER 30

A Royal Priesthood

"Call to Me and I will answer you and tell you great and unsearchable things you do not know."

~ Jeremiah 33:3 ~

As you plead for the great mercies of the new covenant to be bestowed, remember always:

1. The infinite willingness of God to bless: His very nature is a pledge of it. He delights in mercy. He waits to be gracious. His promises and the experience of His saints assure us of it.

2. Why then does the blessing seem to take so long? In creating man with a free will and making him a partner in the rule of the earth, God limited

Himself. He made Himself dependent on what man would do. Man through his prayer holds the measure of what God can do in blessing.

3. Think of how God is hindered and disappointed when His children do not pray or pray only a little. The weak, feeble life of the church, the lack of the power of the Holy Spirit for conversion and holiness, is all due to a lack of prayer. How different the church would be, and how many more people would get saved if God's people called upon Him unceasingly!

4. And yet God has blessed us up to the measure of the faith and the zeal of His people. It is not for them to be content with this, as a sign of His approval, but rather to say, "If He has blessed our feeble efforts and prayers, imagine what He will do if we yield ourselves wholly to a life of intercession!"

5. Repent of and confess the fact that our lack of consecration has kept back God's blessing from the world. He was ready to save people, but we were not willing to live in wholehearted devotion to Christ in His service.

Child of God, God counts on you to take your place before His throne as an intercessor. Realize your holy calling as a royal priesthood.

Begin to live a new life in the assurance that intercession, in both the likeness to and the fellowship with the interceding Lord Jesus in heaven, is the highest privilege an individual can desire. In this spirit take up the word with large expectations, "Call to Me and I will answer you and tell you great and unsearchable things you do not know."

Let each one who has read this far say whether he is willing, whether he is longing to give himself wholly to this blessed calling and, in the power of Jesus Christ, to make intercession, supplication for God's church and people and for a dying world, the one chief object of his life. Is this asking too much?

Is it too much to yield your life for this holy service of the royal priesthood to that blessed Lord who gave Himself for us?

Dear Lord,

Thank You that I can take my place as an intercessor in Your service. Give me the strength to yield my life wholly to You, Jesus.

Amen.

Stand in the gap

Realize your holy calling as an intercessor.

CHAPTER 31

Intercession,
a Divine Reality

*Another angel came ... He was given much incense
to offer, with the prayers of all saints, on the golden
altar before the throne.*

~ Revelation 8:3 ~

Has this little book revealed the low position that
the church has given to intercession? Do you realize
the supreme importance of making it an essential,
indispensable element of Christian life? To those
who take God's Word in its full meaning, there can
be no doubt about the answer.

Intercession is, by amazing grace, an essential

element in God's redeeming purpose – so much so that without it the failure of its accomplishment may lie at our doors.

Christ's intercession in heaven is essential to His carrying out of the work He began upon earth, but He calls for the intercession of the saints in the attainment of His object.

Just think of what we read, "All this from God, who reconciled us to Himself through Christ and gave us the ministry of reconciliation" (2 Cor. 5:18). As the reconciliation was dependent on Christ's doing His part, so in the accomplishment of the work He calls on the church to do her part.

We see how Paul regarded constant intercession as indispensable to the fulfillment of the work that had been entrusted to him. It is but one aspect of that mighty power of God, which works in the heart of His believing people. Intercession is indeed a divine reality.

Without it the church loses one of its chief beauties and loses the joy and the power that the Spirit life has to achieve great things for God.

Without it, the command to preach the gospel to every creature can never be carried out.

Without it, there is no power for the church to recover from her weak, inconsequential existence and conquer the world. And in the life of the believer, minister, or member, there can be no entrance into the abundant life and joy of daily fellowship with

God, except as he takes his place among God's elect – the watchmen and remembrances of God, who cry to Him day and night.

Church of Christ, awake, awake! Listen to the call, "Pray continually" (1 Thess. 5:17). Take no rest, and give God no rest. Let the answer be, even if it is with a sigh, "For Zion's sake I will not keep silent" (Isa. 62:1).

God's Spirit will reveal to us the power of a life of intercession as a divine reality, an essential and indispensable element of the great redemption and the true Christian life.

May God help us to know and to fulfill our calling!

Stand in the gap

Pray continually!
